YOUR PASSPORT TO

PORTUGAL

by Nancy Dickmann

CAPSTONE PRESS
a capstone imprint

Published by Capstone Press, an imprint of Capstone
1710 Roe Crest Drive, North Mankato, Minnesota 56003
capstonepub.com

Library of Congress Cataloging-in-Publication Data is available on the Library
of Congress website.
ISBN: 9781669058540 (hardcover)
ISBN: 9781669058496 (paperback)
ISBN: 9781669058502 (ebook PDF)

Summary: What is it like to live in or visit Portugal? What makes Portugal's
culture unique? Explore the geography, traditions, and daily lives of
Portuguese people.

Editorial Credits
Editor: Carrie Sheely; Designer: Bobbie Nuytten; Media Researcher: Rebekah
Hubstenberger; Production Specialist: Whitney Schaefer

Image Credits
Alamy: Hemis, 10, IanDagnall Computing, 6; Capstone Press: Eric Gohl, 5;
Getty Images: Alexander Spatari, 16 (bottom right), Carol Yepes, 16 (bottom
left), iStock/PRG-Estudio, 14, iStock/zanskar, 9, Joe Regan, 7, Rita Franca/
SOPA Images/LightRocket, 23; Shutterstock: Danita Delimont, 25, Dmytro
Surkov, 22, iacomino FRiMAGES, 13, leoks, 19, leonori, 17, RossHelen, 20, Sean
Pavone, Cover (bottom), Sopotnicki, 29, Traxparent Wildlife, 12, Tsuguliev, 15,
Vlad1988, 27

Design Elements
Shutterstock: Flipser, Gil C (flag), GRADIENT BACKGROUND (map), Net
Vector, pingebat, Yevhenii Dubinko

Printed and bound in China.   PO 5593

CONTENTS

Words in **bold** are in the glossary.

CHAPTER ONE

WELCOME TO PORTUGAL!

People sit outside at a café. They chat and sip coffee. The buildings around them are brightly colored. Their balconies look out over cobblestone streets. Yellow trams drive up and down hills. In the distance is the Atlantic Ocean. Sunlight sparkles on the water. This scene is in Lisbon, the charming capital city of Portugal.

Portugal is at the western edge of Europe. More than 10 million people live there. Portugal has many historic buildings. It also has natural beauty. Tourists come to visit its beautiful beaches. People enjoy comfortable summers and mild winters in Portugal.

MAP OF PORTUGAL

Inset

Sintra-Cascais Natural Park

Castle of the Moors

▲● Sintra

Pena Palace

Belém Tower △

■ LISBON

Porto ●   Douro River

PORTUGAL

Tagus River

See inset

● Évora

N

W — E

S

■ Capital City

● City

△ Landmark

■ Sintra-Cascais Natural Park

Explore Portugal's cities and landmarks.

SAILORS AND EXPLORERS

Portugal has a long coast. Sailing has always been an important part of Portuguese culture. In the 1400s, Portuguese sailors began to explore. Bartolomeu Dias sailed around the southern tip of Africa in 1488. Ten years later, Vasco da Gama went to India. In the 1500s, Pedro Álvares Cabral reached Brazil. Ferdinand Magellan sailed to India and Africa. He later sailed for Spain.

Bartolomeu Dias

FACT FILE

OFFICIAL NAME: .... PORTUGUESE REPUBLIC
POPULATION: 10,296,000
LAND AREA: .... 35,556 SQ. MI. (92,090 SQ KM)
CAPITAL: .... LISBON
MONEY: .... EURO
GOVERNMENT: .... SEMI-PRESIDENTIAL REPUBLIC
LANGUAGES: .... PORTUGUESE AND MIRANDESE

GEOGRAPHY: To the west and south, Portugal borders the Atlantic Ocean. Portugal borders Spain to the east and north. It also includes several islands.

NATURAL RESOURCES: Portugal has copper, tin, lithium, and stone such as marble. Farmers raise livestock and grow tomatoes, olives, and grapes.

The Monument to the Discoveries in Lisbon reminds people of the Portuguese explorers who made important discoveries.

CHAPTER TWO

HISTORY OF PORTUGAL

Humans lived in Portugal about 35,000 years ago. Portugal's early people lived simple lives. They hunted and gathered food to eat. Later, they began to farm.

People in Portugal started to make bronze tools about 4,000 years ago. Bronze is a mix of copper and tin. Portugal has a great deal of both of these metals. People traded the metals and received different goods in return.

FACT

The Portuguese language is based on Latin. Romans brought the Latin language to Portugal.

INVASIONS

Portugal has been invaded many times. The Romans took over in about 140 BCE. The Romans built roads, bridges, and many present-day cities. In the early 400s, Germanic tribes attacked.

In 711, **Muslim** troops from North Africa invaded. **Christians** in Portugal fought back. Fighting continued for hundreds of years. Eventually, the Muslims were pushed out. In 1139, Afonso Henriques became Portugal's first king.

A statue of Afonso Henriques stands in Guimarães, Portugal.

Beginning in the 1400s, the Portuguese took land in Africa, India, and Brazil to set up **colonies**. They kidnapped people from Africa and enslaved them to work in the colonies. Portugal's rulers sent many enslaved people to work in the Brazil colony.

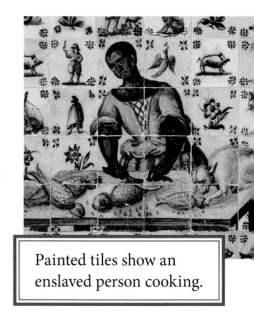

Painted tiles show an enslaved person cooking.

In 1580, Portugal became part of Spain. The Spanish ruled Portugal until 1640.

KINGS AND DEMOCRACY

In 1755, an earthquake destroyed most of Lisbon. Around the same time, Portugal's power started to fade. In 1822, the colony of Brazil broke away.

By the 1900s, many people in Portugal wanted a **democracy**. In 1910, they got their wish. But their way of life didn't improve. António de Oliveira Salazar became the prime minister in 1932. He ruled as a **dictator**.

TIMELINE OF PORTUGUESE HISTORY

ABOUT 35,000 BCE: Hunter-gatherers live in Portugal.

ABOUT 2000 BCE: People in Portugal start using bronze.

ABOUT 140 BCE: Romans invade and take over Portugal.

400s CE: Germanic tribes invade Portugal.

711: Muslim troops invade.

1420s: Prince Henry encourages Portuguese sailors to explore the world. He is later known as Henry the Navigator.

1580–1640: Spain rules Portugal.

1755: An earthquake destroys Lisbon.

1822: Brazil becomes independent from Portugal.

1910: Portugal changes from a monarchy to a democracy.

1916–1918: Portugal joins World War I on the side of the Allies.

1939–1945: Portugal stays neutral in World War II.

1974: Portugal's dictator is toppled.

1986: Portugal joins the group that later becomes the European Union.

2017: A Portuguese politician, António Guterres, becomes secretary-general of the United Nations.

MODERN PORTUGAL

Portugal became a democracy again after a **revolution** in 1974. In 1986, Portugal joined a group that became the European Union. Today, Portugal works with other European countries. It keeps ties with former colonies and has growing businesses.

CHAPTER THREE

EXPLORE PORTUGAL

Portugal is a small country. But it has many landscapes. Rivers have carved out deep valleys. There are marshes where rivers meet the sea. The northern part of the country has tall mountains and thick forests. In the south, the land is flatter. Farmers grow olives, figs, and grapes on the rolling **plains**. The north has a warm climate. It is hotter in the south.

SAND AND SEA

Portugal's coast stretches for nearly 600 miles (966 kilometers). Steep cliffs tower above sandy beaches. Sand dunes are home to birds such as red kites. Powerful waves pound the shore. Their force has carved out caves in the coastal rocks. The waves are great for surfing.

Red kites are red-brown with forked tails.

Waves formed the Benagil Cave in southern Portugal.

Many people enjoy visiting Portugal's parks. One of the most visited national parks is Sintra-Cascais Natural Park. While there, visitors can climb up to the Castle of the Moors.

FACT

Two groups of volcanic islands are part of Portugal. They are in the Atlantic Ocean. Madeira is near the African coast. The Azores are farther out at sea.

A terraced hillside with grapevines creates a unique pattern in the Douro Valley.

THE DOURO VALLEY

The Douro River flows across northern Portugal. Tall hills rise along both sides of the river. The Douro Valley is perfect for growing grapes. Farmers have cut **terraces** into the hillsides. The grapevines make them look like green steps. Tourists often take boat or train trips along the Douro.

CASTLES AND CATHEDRALS

Portugal is full of historic buildings. Some are hundreds of years old. Castles stand on many hilltops. Workers built them long ago to protect the land from invaders. Now some of them are hotels. Portugal also has many churches and **cathedrals**. Some have painted tiles on the walls.

MOUNTAIN RETREAT

Portuguese kings sometimes spent time during summers at the mountaintop retreat of Sintra. It has palaces, castles, and gardens. Pena Palace was completed in 1854. It stands on the ruins of an old **monastery**. Its towers and bright colors make it look like something from a fairy tale.

BUSY CITIES

Lisbon is Portugal's capital and largest city. It is in southern Portugal where the Tagus River meets the sea. Most of the city had to be rebuilt after the earthquake in 1755.

Lisbon has an old-fashioned feel. Buildings with red-tiled roofs surround large open plazas. There are museums, theaters, and concert halls. Many people enjoy riding a tall elevator called the Elevador de Santa Justa to get majestic views of the city. People also visit Belém Tower. Built in the early 1500s, it became a World Heritage Site in 1983.

The Elevador de Santa Justa stands 147 feet (45 meters) tall.

The Belém Tower was built to help defend Lisbon's port from attacking ships.

Porto is the second largest city. It lies on the north coast near the mouth of the Douro River. Brightly painted buildings cluster along the riverbank.

Évora is a good place to see Portugal's historical buildings. It has a Roman temple and a castle built by the Moors. The University of Évora was founded in 1559. It is the second oldest university in Portugal.

FACT

Many buildings in Portugal are covered in painted tiles. They are called azulejos. The National Tile Museum in Lisbon is dedicated to them.

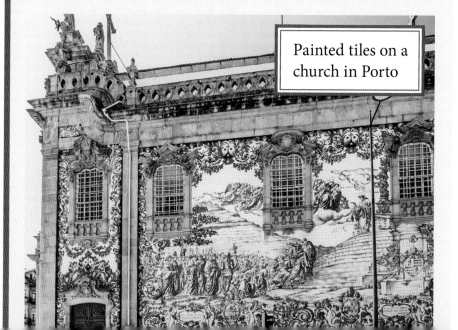

Painted tiles on a church in Porto

CHAPTER FOUR

DAILY LIFE

More than half of Portugal's people live in cities. People enjoy shopping and going to restaurants. In rural areas, people live in villages. Many of them work on farms. Some raise pigs and chickens. Others grow crops such as oranges, olives, and corn.

Most Portuguese people are Christians. Of these, most are Catholic. Religion is an important part of Portuguese life.

SCHOOL

About 100 years ago, most Portuguese people couldn't read. In 1952, the government made a law that all children must go to school. Now nearly everyone can read. Children go to school until age 18. They learn Portuguese, math, science, and history. They also learn English. About a quarter of Portuguese people can speak English.

A mountainside village in Portugal has tightly packed buildings.

FOOD AND DRINK

Food is a big part of Portuguese culture. Lunch is usually the main meal. People also have an afternoon snack time called *lanche*. It may include juice or coffee and a sandwich or cake. It can be sweet or savory.

Seafood is very common in Portugal. People often eat octopus or sardines. Dried, salted cod is cooked in different ways.

Many meals include meat. People eat chicken with a spicy chili sauce. It comes from lands in Africa that Portugal once ruled. A meat sandwich is a popular fast-food meal. It's served with melted cheese and tomato sauce.

Portuguese people enjoy sweet treats too. Vanilla-flavored custard tarts are popular.

People can buy a traditional meat sandwich called a francesinha in Porto.

CHOCOLATE SALAMI

Don't be fooled—this sweet treat has no meat! It's a mixture of chocolate and cookie pieces that looks like salami.

Ingredients:
- 7 ounces dark chocolate
- 6 tablespoons butter
- 1/3 cup sugar
- 2 pasteurized eggs
- 1/2 teaspoon vanilla
- 7 ounces Maria biscuits, broken into pieces
  (Graham crackers or vanilla wafers may also be used.)
- wax paper
- string
- 2 tablespoons powdered sugar

Instructions:

1. Put the butter and chocolate in a heatproof bowl and melt in the microwave. Heat in 20-second bursts and stir regularly. (It will turn lumpy if you overheat it.)
2. In another bowl, beat the sugar, eggs, and vanilla.
3. Stir the egg mixture into the melted chocolate a little at a time.
4. Stir in the cookie pieces. Then let the mixture cool for about 10 minutes.
5. Cut two pieces of wax paper and put half the mixture on each.
6. Roll each "salami" into a thick tube. Twist the ends and tie with string.
7. Refrigerate for at least 2 hours. Then unwrap the rolls, dust them with powdered sugar, and cut into slices.

CHAPTER FIVE

HOLIDAYS AND CELEBRATIONS

Catholics in Portugal celebrate important religious holidays. Before Easter, people often clean their homes. Then a priest blesses the homes. On Easter, families often share a meal of goat or lamb. They eat special bread called folar. It often has boiled eggs baked into it and a cross shape on top.

Christmas is an important holiday. On Christmas Eve, many families share cod, potatoes, and fruit cake.

FACT

Many Portuguese set out nativity scenes before Christmas. They set them up in their homes and in public places such as town squares.

CARNIVALS AND SAINTS

Lent is a period of fasting before Easter. Just before it starts, many cities have big carnivals. People wear costumes and dance in parades.

Some festivals honor Catholic saints. In June, the São João festival celebrates John the Baptist. In Porto, people used to hit each other with leeks during the celebration. Now they use squeaky plastic hammers instead. In Braga, there are plays and candlelit processions.

A dancer performs at a carnival in Ovar, Portugal.

NATIONAL HOLIDAYS

Portuguese people have holidays to celebrate their history. April 25 is Freedom Day. People remember the revolution in 1974. June 10 is Portugal Day. It celebrates Luís de Camões, a famous poet who died on this day in 1580. On October 5, people celebrate the beginning of democracy in Portugal. The end of Spanish rule is remembered on December 1.

MORE TRADITIONS

Portugal has other traditions. On June 12, Catholics remember a fish that is said to have listened to Saint Anthony. People eat sardines. Men give women love poems tucked into basil plants.

The Festival of the Trays takes place in Tomar. It is held every four years in July. People walk through the streets. Women and girls wear huge headdresses. They are made of paper flowers and stacks of bread.

Women wear headdresses during the Festival of the Trays. The trays are usually built to be as tall as the people carrying them.

CHAPTER SIX

SPORTS AND RECREATION

Many Portuguese people enjoy watching and playing sports. Soccer is by far the most popular. People play it for fun. They cheer for their favorite teams. The Portuguese men's national team is very good. They often qualify for the World Cup. In 2016, the Portugal soccer team won the European Championship.

Basketball, volleyball, and other sports are popular too. Many people enjoy playing a team sport called handball. Teams of seven try to pass the ball and throw it into the other team's goal.

Many people take part in water sports. Surfing, sailing, kite surfing, and scuba diving are popular.

Cristiano Ronaldo of the Portugal national soccer team plays in a match.

JOGO DE CABRA CEGA

The Portuguese name for this game means "blind goat game." It's similar to another group game called blindman's buff.

1. Choose one player to be the "blind goat" and put a blindfold on them.
2. The remaining players form a circle, holding hands. The goat is in the middle of the circle.
3. The goat turns around three times while the other players chant to tease them. The goat then begins to chase the other players, who can spread out to escape.
4. If the goat catches someone, they try to guess who it is. If they guess right, the two players swap roles.

MUSIC AND DANCE

Fado is a style of traditional Portuguese music. Even though many fado songs are about love, they are sad. Different regions have different styles. Many young singers perform it in a modern style.

A fado singer performs in Lisbon.

Folk dancing is popular in Portugal. Couples often perform these dances. They wear colorful costumes. They twirl and snap their fingers. Musicians play guitars, tambourines, and accordions. One popular dance is the fandango. Another, the vira, is danced in a circle.

SOMETHING FOR EVERYONE

Portugal is a beautiful country. Its history is full of struggle and change, but the Portuguese spirit stays strong. Portugal is known around the world for its food, beaches, and music. From rivers to mountains, there is something for everyone to enjoy.

GLOSSARY

**cathedral
(cah-THEE-drul)**
an important church
building that is run by
a bishop

**Christian
(KRIS-chuhn)**
a person who follows
a religion based on the
teachings of Jesus Christ

colony (KAH-luh-nee)
a territory settled by people
from another country and
controlled by that country

**democracy
(di-MAH-kruh-see)**
a form of government
in which the citizens can
choose their leaders

dictator (DIK-tay-tuhr)
a ruler who has complete
power and often rules
harshly

**monastery
(MAH-nuh-ster-ee)**
a group of buildings where
monks live and work

Muslim (MUHZ-luhm)
a follower of the religion
of Islam

plain (PLAYN)
a large, flat area of land with
few trees

**revolution
(rev-uh-LOO-shun)**
an uprising by a group of
people against a system of
government or a way of life

terrace (TER-iss)
a ridge made in a hillside

READ MORE

Allen, Jules. *Portugal vs. Spain*. North Mankato: Capstone, 2023.

Blauer, Ettagale, and Jason Lauré. *Portugal*. New York: Children's Press, 2019.

Costa Knufinke, Joana. *Europe*. New York: Children's Press, 2019.

INTERNET SITES

Kiddle: Portugal Facts for Kids
kids.kiddle.co/Portugal

National Geographic Kids: Portugal
kids.nationalgeographic.com/geography/countries/article/portugal

U.S. News and World Report: Portugal
usnews.com/news/best-countries/portugal

INDEX

ABOUT THE AUTHOR

Nancy Dickmann grew up reading encyclopedias for fun, and after many years working in children's publishing, she now has her dream job as a full-time author. She has had more than 200 titles published so far, mainly on science topics. She finds that the best part of the job is researching and learning new things. One highlight was getting to interview a real astronaut about using the toilet in space!

SELECT BOOKS IN THIS SERIES

YOUR PASSPORT TO **AUSTRALIA**
YOUR PASSPORT TO **BRAZIL**
YOUR PASSPORT TO **CANADA**
YOUR PASSPORT TO **CUBA**
YOUR PASSPORT TO **ENGLAND**

YOUR PASSPORT TO **GERMANY**
YOUR PASSPORT TO **JAPAN**
YOUR PASSPORT TO **MEXICO**
YOUR PASSPORT TO **SAUDI ARABIA**
YOUR PASSPORT TO **SOUTH AFRICA**